Calm and
EASY COLOR

THIS BOOK BELONGS TO

_____

_____

Coloring Tip

Colored pencils, alcohol-based markers, and other wet mediums all suit Amazon's selection of paper. However, is recommended to place an extra sheet of paper behind the page you are coloring to avoid any possible bleed-through.

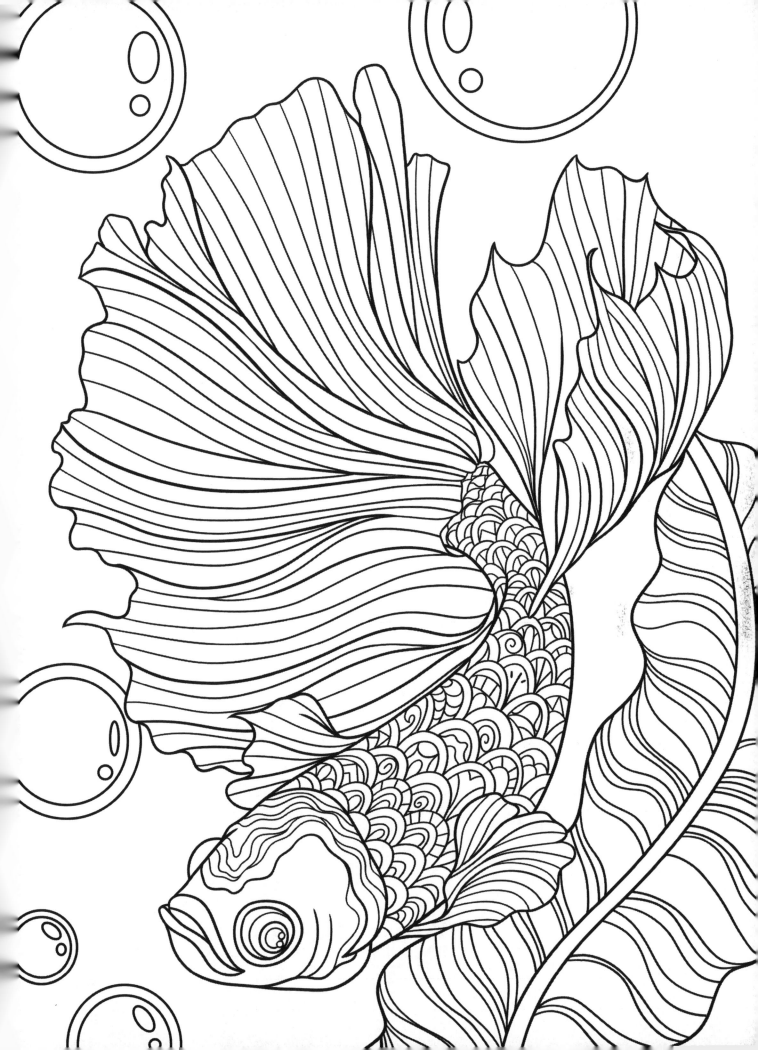

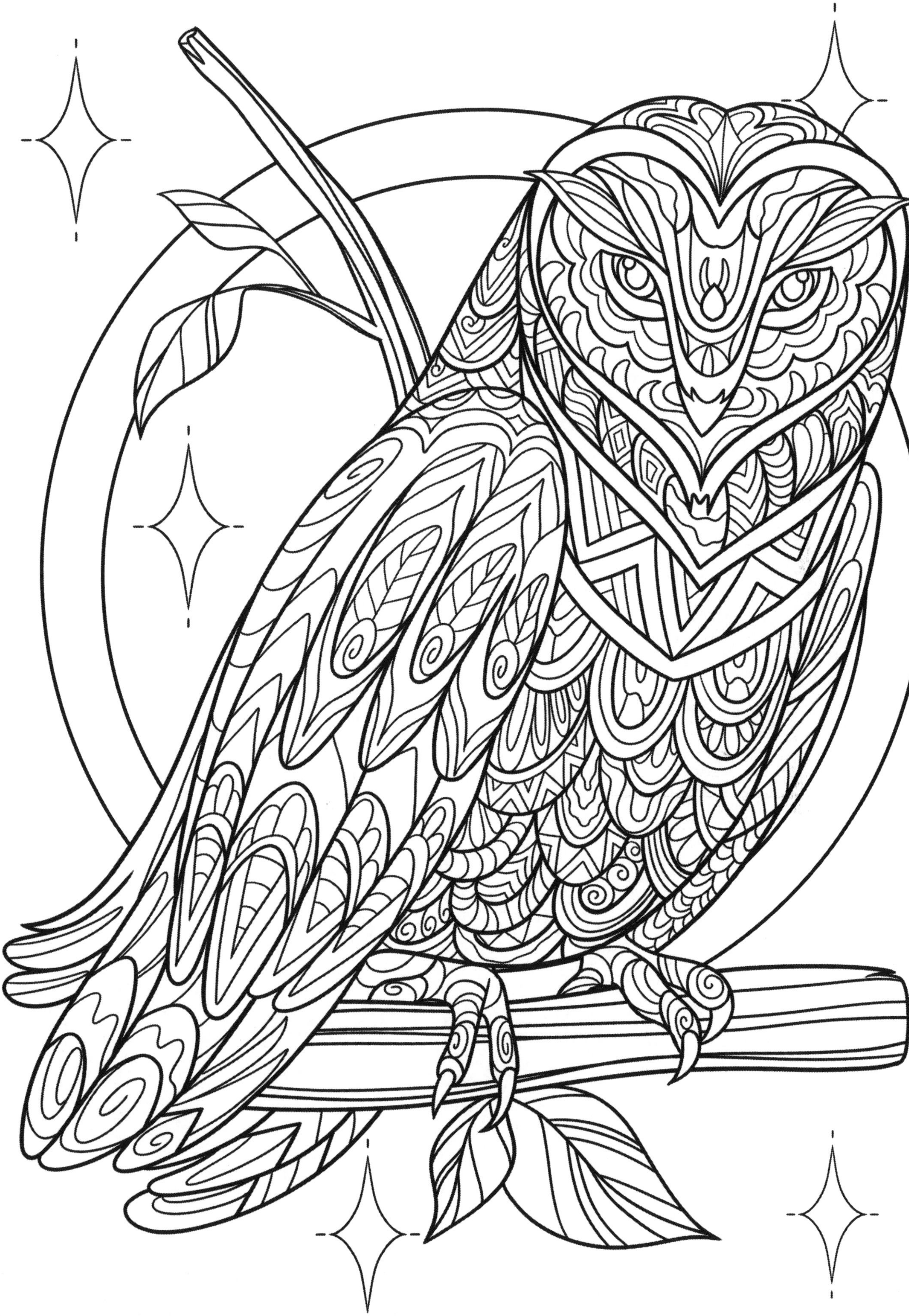

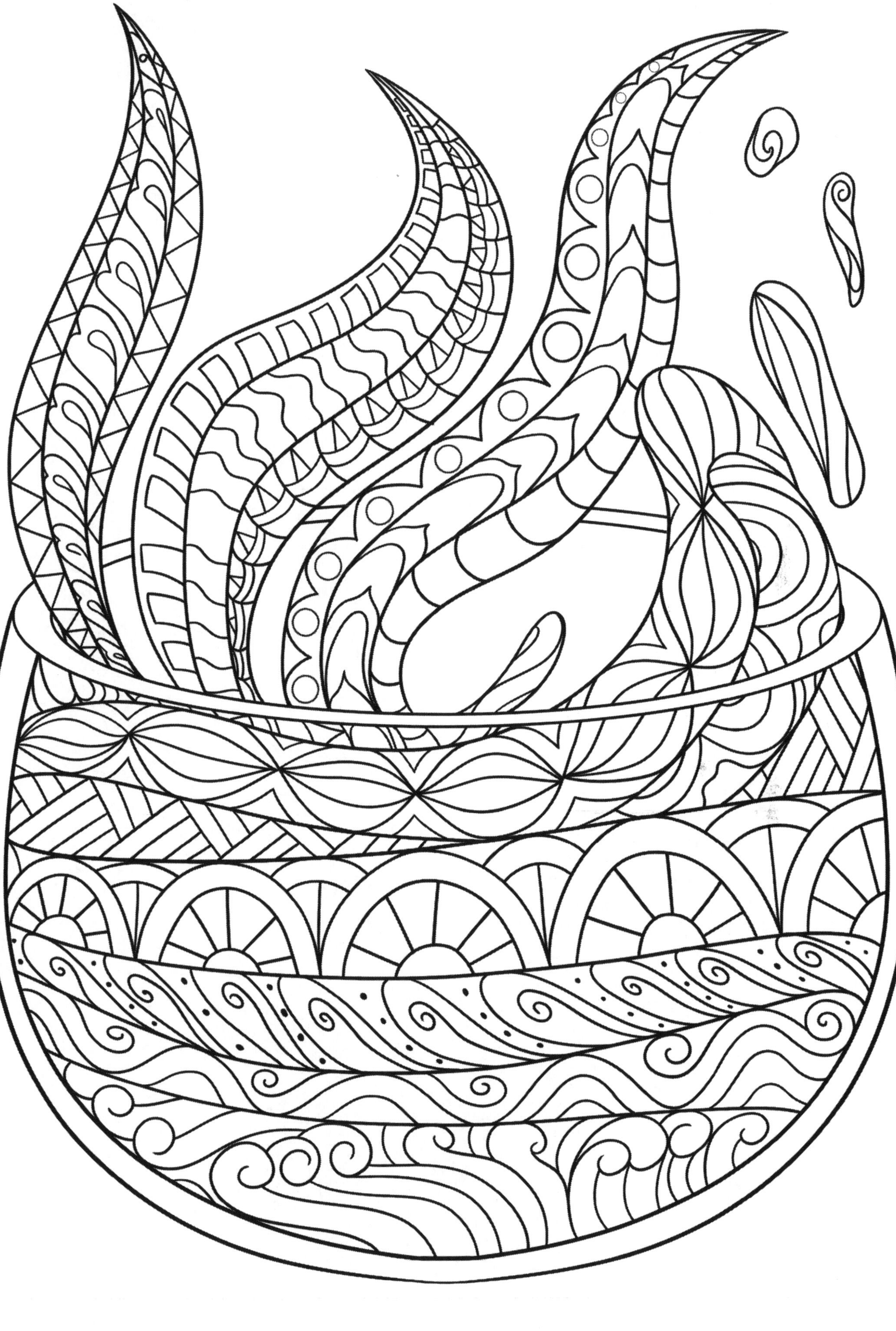

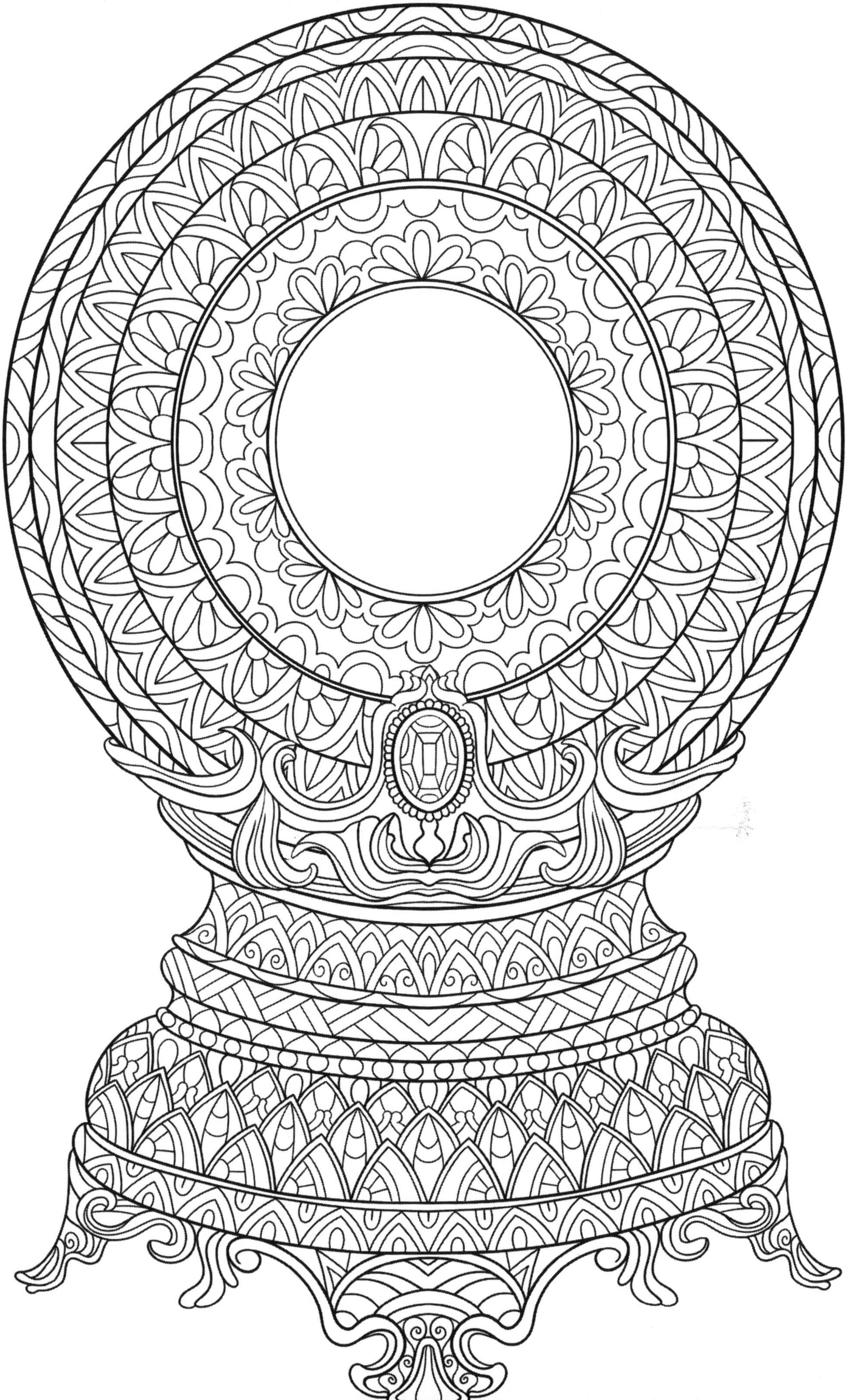

TEST COLOR PAGE

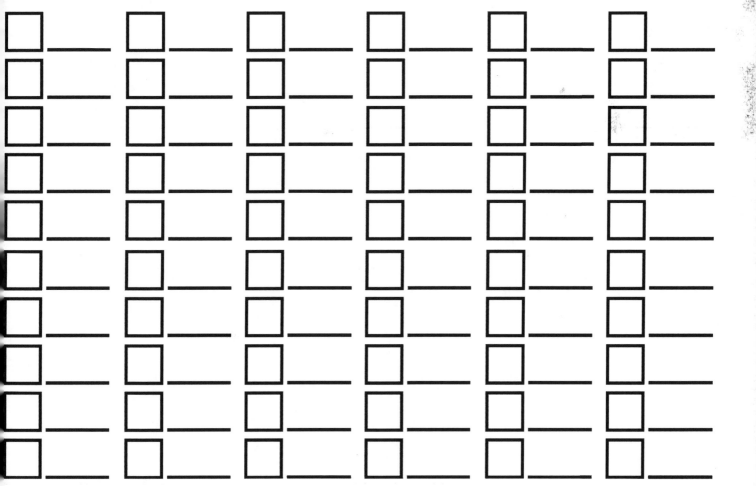

TEST COLOR PAGE

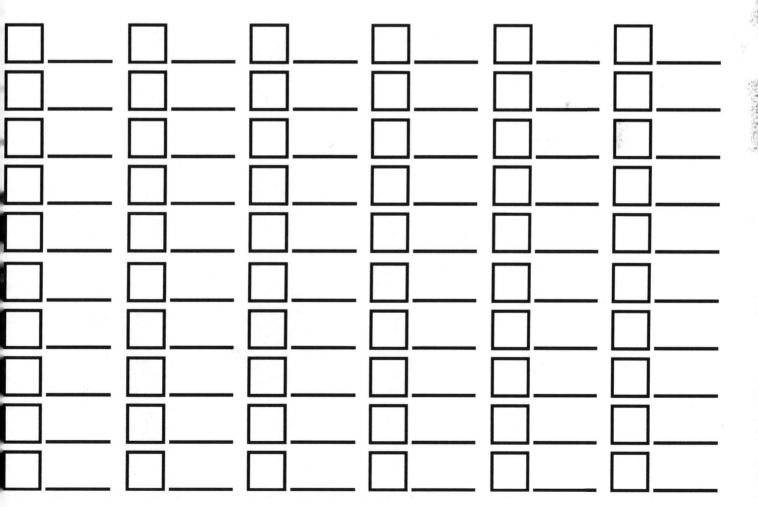

TEST COLOR PAGE

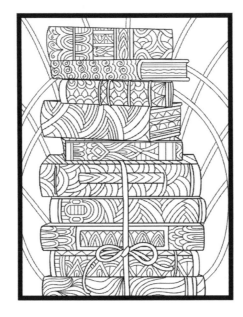

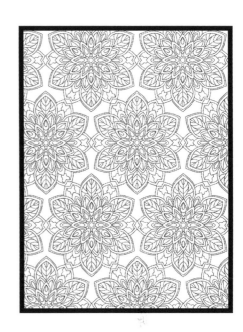

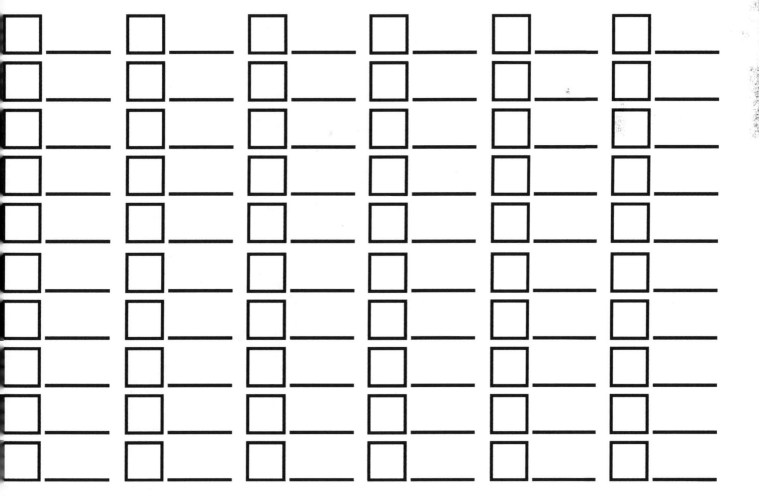

A Greeting from 99 OWL

Thank you so much! Your being here means the world to us.

It is always a pleasure for us when you trust 99OWL coloring books. Your support allows us to pursue our dream of being a professional brand. Thus, we are always willing to receive your valuable feedback which brings us a better understanding of customer satisfaction and motivation to create more excellent artwork every single day.

99OWL – where colors bloom and shine!

Coloring is more than just a recreational pastime. To us, it is a healing activity that can help relieve stress and anxiety, allowing everyone to immerse in the art and spread imagination. So let 99OWL become a passionate buddy on your journey of conquering the true color of your life.

Feel free to check us out

It truly brings us joy to see your finished masterpieces!
Please tag #99owl #99owlcoloring

---

mail: coloring@99owl.com

Made in the USA
Columbia, SC
05 July 2023

20057449R00046